PUMPING PLASTIC: The Jump Rope Fitness Plan

PUMPING PLASTIC

THE JUMP ROPE FITNESS PLAN

By John Cassidy
Illustrated by Diane Waller
Klutz Press • Palo Alto, California

Published by
Klutz Press
Post Office Box 2992
Stanford, CA 94305

ISBN 0-932592-06-6

Individual copies of this book as well as assorted flying apparatus may be ordered directly from the publisher. See back pages for details.

At its best, life should be a series of little ups and downs.

— *Calvin Coolidge*

THIS BOOK IS GOING TO TRY TO GET YOU TO interrupt your normal day's activities, today and for the rest of your life, and jump up and down, for what will initially seem like a terribly long time, over a rope you will be swinging under your feet.

Recognizing that there will be some readers with an initial reluctance to this idea, I've begun with a section entitled "Why Bother?". In it I have used scientific fact, clinical studies, medieval superstition, child psychology, a number of half-truths, and the occasional bald-faced lie.

I stoop to these unfortunate means not only because I feel comfortable with them, but also because of my belief that a person's reluctance to do that which he knows is good for him, springs from an older, rundown section of his brain where strong-arm tactics may be the only option.

I'm also guilty of some ends-justifying-the-means thinking, because the end *here* is nothing less than life itself — in this case, yours.

Jumping rope is a pure aerobic exercise, like jogging, swimming, or cycling. How good an aerobic exercise, what muscles it develops, and in what ways it differs from the rest, I'll describe in detail a bit further on. Suffice it to say for now that jumping rope is an extraordinarily compact, efficient way to develop the cardiovascular efficiency that is the goal of all aerobic exercise.

In the meantime, I have a more basic topic:

1

WHY BOTHER?

So my doctor tells me to get out there and start jogging. Tells me it'll add ten years to my life. I didn't believe him, but the other day I tried it and sure enough, when I got back to the house, I felt ten years older.

An old joke.

2

The American "fitness boom" is now about 25 years old, having started, like as not, in Dwight Eisenhower's golf cart. Hardly a man is now alive who can recall the time when fluorescent striped shoes and nylon shorts were not seen upon these shores. And to the casual observer, seeing our herds of joggers and legions of tennis ball swatters, it might seem as if the boom were still in full swing.

But the evidence suggests otherwise:

• A 1980 U.S. Department of Health and Human Sciences study reviewed a number of polls and reported that 65% of the adult population fails to exercise either regularly or vigorously enough to maintain minimum standards of physical fitness.

• A 1982 study of 4 million schoolchildren disclosed the fact that 57% of them were unable to perform to the standards "reasonably expected of a healthy schoolchild".

• Twenty percent of the population is, according to the National Center of Health Statistics, "significantly over-weight."

• The most telling statistic of all of course is in the frequency of American heart attacks: every fifth man has one before the age of 60. And when he does, he suffers from a disease that does not exist for three-fourths of the world's population.

The culprit, to no one's particular surprise, lies fairly close to the center of the American Way of Life — as practiced in the nation's lawn furniture and fast food outlets. Why it is that an otherwise very attractive hammock and yummy burger should have anything to do with one's cardiovascular health is something that requires a bit of background understanding.

3

THE BODY HUMAN

Although no one who's never lived in one has ever been asked, it's an almost universally held belief that the human body is a Marvelous Machine. That may be so, but even a beginner's understanding of the heart and vascular system would have to lead one to conclude that it is also a plumber's nightmare. In order to feed and fuel each additional pound of us, The Contractor has found it necessary to install one *mile* of blood vessels.

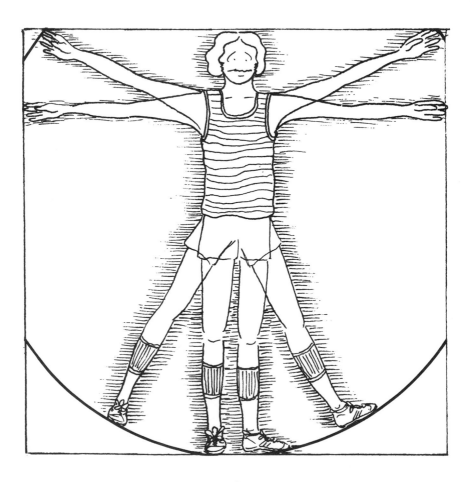

This is efficiency?

To get some idea of what this means, take as an example a relatively normal human being, male, owner of one of these Marvelous Machines who weighs, say, 175 pounds and lives in a suburb of San Francisco, say about 35 miles south.

By means of an involved computation, it turns out that he owns and operates some 175 miles of major hemoglobic highways and byways. The anatomy textbook he holds before him informs him that he irrigates each and every one of these miles not daily, not hourly, but approximately once every minute.

The weight of these realizations staggers him. The idea of *driving* 175 miles exhausts him, never mind pumping them.

He looks at a map. He assumes he's pumping north. San Francisco . . . Marin County . . . Santa Rosa . . . here it is, Ft. Bragg. He's only been to Ft. Bragg once, but, if memory serves, it *was* a long way. Not the kind of jaunt you'd normally want to make 1440 times a day.

Leaving our hypothetical example to himself for a while, to recover from these discoveries, we'll take a closer look at the engine behind all this.

MY FAVORITE ORGAN

Among all the organs, and I'm trying to be as objective as I can about this, I think my favorite is the heart. Some will say the liver, of course, and point to its ornithine decarboxylase synthesis function, and others will prefer the pituitary gland, nestled up there by the hypothalmus. But for my money, you just can't beat the heart as a team player. A simple organ with simple needs. Hardworking,

5

always on the job, and, given the extremely repetitive nature of its task, very uncomplaining.

I have only one concern. As any astronaut, test pilot or engineer will tell you, the secret to reliability, when it comes to marvelous machinery, is *redundancy*. A DC-10 for example, can fly on one engine. It has three. The space shuttle has 3 separate systems for lowering its landing gear and 5 computers. All of them completely independent.

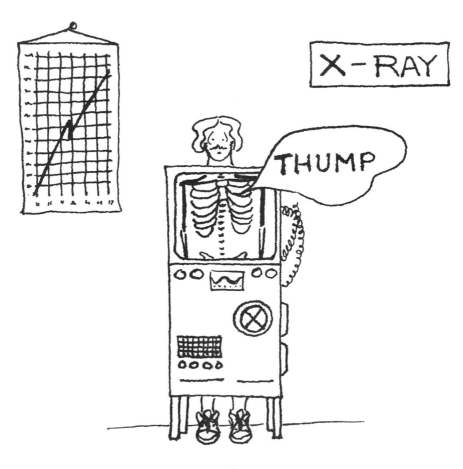

None of this strikes anyone as extravagant. Who wants to take chances with all that money?

Now consider your own fragile mortality and the number of chances you're eager to take with it. Surely, one would think, The Contractor would use as much caution and wisdom in design as Lockheed or United Technologies.

But no. In vain does one search for some version of a cardiac pinch hitter. Not even a spare part.

The principle of back-up system seems so extraordinarily reasonable that its absence in the field of human anatomy strikes me, at least, as an appalling oversight. But the fact of it leads to only one reasonable conclusion: Since we've been forced to carry all of our cardiac eggs in one basket, it behooves us to take marvelous good care of that basket.

Which brings us back to the heart and the principle that underlies much of its proper care and feeding.

Use It Or Lose It

Popular descriptions of the heart almost always rely on the automotive metaphor: the heart as sturdy little V-2, chugging along on 60cc displacement. But the image has a flaw. Parking your car is great automotive care. Garage the thing and it'll outlast your children's children. But park your heart and you're asking for trouble. It thrives on use.

The difference between you and the family station wagon is locked up in the nature of cellular regeneration. If you apply a steady environmental pressure to a living organism, it will make an adaptation. In the case of your heart-muscle, if the "pressure" is aerobic exercise, the adaptation will be strength and efficiency. More blood containing more oxygen will be pumped on fewer strokes, through wider vessels, into more fully inflated lungs.

You will be, in short, a better animal.

This is not, incidentally, advertising copy from the jogging wear industry. These are physical changes that a condi-

7

tioned body undergoes and they've been exhaustively documented by a generation of research.

But as long as the subject's been raised, it seems a shame not to list at least a fraction of the less documented claims, beginning with those that have a great deal of supporting evidence and ending with my favorites, those that have practically none.

• **The Jane Fonda Look.** Aerobic exercise burns fat, whether it be located in thick thighs, bulging bottoms or mega-midriffs. A diet without lasting commitment to aerobic exercise is a well-worn path of frustration to short-term losses and long-term gains.

- **More Social Security Benefits.** Heart disease is America's No. 1 killer of men between the ages of 34 and 69 and Number 2 for women in the same age group. One of the primary suspects is that American dietary favorite, cholesterol. There is strong evidence that aerobic exercise both decreases the level of "bad" cholesterol (low-density lipoproteins to you or me) at the same time it increases the level of "good" cholesterol (high-density lipoproteins). "Good" cholesterol got its name, incidentally, from an association with lowered cardiovascular death rates, an apparent result of its scavenger effect on "bad" cholesterol deposits on artery walls.

- **More Energy.** Probably the most common justification used by regular exercisers. A conditioning program builds up a reserve of muscle power and stamina that everyday life makes a decreasingly small dent in. The result is your own private energy glut.

- **An Intolerable Degree of Self-Satisfaction.** This is another well-documented consequence of regular exercise, probably the result of questionable self-analysis: "I'm working so hard to take care of myself, I must have something really special to take care of!"
    Despite its faulty logic, and the fact that it gets old quickly for those around you, still, it's a nice pick-me-up.

- **Better Social Life.** Almost guaranteed. You'll be working under delusions of grandeur (see above) and making use of some deadly opening lines ("Mind if I check your resting pulse rate?") You can't lose.

So ends my pitch. But before I go ahead and close the sale, I realize you have a right to check my sources. After all, why should you take my word for it?

WHO DO YOU TRUST?

The Medical Community?

The American College of Sports Medicine is an organization of 10,000 physicians and researchers who specialize in the health consequences of physical exercise. Their Position Statement on the value of aerobic exercise may be considered the definitive word on the subject from the mainstream of Western medical thought. After reviewing approximately 600 studies done over a period of more than 30 years, examining tens of thousands of subjects, their conclusion was unequivocal: regular aerobic exercise of a minimum intensity has an unquestionably positive effect on the health of the heart and vascular system.

How about medical quacks?

Juan Blanche is a Filipino medicine man with a reputation for unaesthesized surgery from across the room. As part of his overall health care plan, Juan suggests a diet heavy on the chicken brains and betel nut and a regimen of vigorous walking.

Faith Healers?

The Reverend James T. Clew, who in his hey-day, helped more cripples throw away their crutches than most, used to prescribe a strict program of faith, frequent ice baths, a light diet of greens — and plenty of open-air exercise.

The Life Insurance Industry?

The Equitable Life Insurance Company offers reduced rates to policy holders who claim to be regular exercisers who do not smoke. The practice would undoubtedly be more widespread within the industry were it not for the credibility problem insurance companies have with client-reported health habits.

10

The Health Tonic Industry?

Adolphus Hohensee, author of *Your Personality Glands* and successful promoter and lecturer of the late 1940's, tirelessly extolled the virtues of exercise — along with a heavy dose of Hohensee Vigortonic® and a strict diet of produce grown on the Hohensee Fit-Farm. Good for whatever ailed you.

To continue on in this vein is to run the risk of becoming a nag, and so I will leave with just a few words of advice from Dr. Per-Olaf Astrand, an internationally known Swedish physiologist who suggests that those opting for a sedentary life of TV and pinochle first pass a rigorous physical "to establish whether one's state of health is good enough to stand the inactivity."

For the rest of you, I have a modest proposal:

11

JUMP UP AND DOWN

Dr. Kenneth Cooper, author of *Aerobics* and *The Aerobics Way*, who has done as much field research in exercise physiology as anyone in the U.S., has evaluated 31 activities for their value as aerobic exercise. They range from running to fencing to boxing. Each has been assigned "aerobic points" based on the stress they place on the cardiovascular system. Jumping rope, according to this scheme, if it's done for 10 minutes at a moderate pace, is equivalent to: running one mile in twelve minutes, cycling two miles in six minutes, swimming a quarter of a mile in twelve minutes, playing twenty minutes of handball, two sets of tennis, or eighteen holes of golf.

In response to the question which everyone asks at this point, "But which is the *best* exercise?", scientists have tended to shrug their shoulders since each of them has its advantages and disadvantages.

Somebody has got to know the answer though and in this case, fortunately, it turns out to be me.

It's simple. The best exercise is the one you'll do.

You're a curling fanatic? Fine. An hour or so five times a week should do you fine. Backyard Badminton? Better figure on about twenty hours a week. Disco? Five hours.

The time estimates are from Cooper's studies, but the underlying principle that exercise has to be taken in a minimum quantity and at a minimum intensity to be beneficial has been established by nearly every researcher in the field. Thursday night bowling just doesn't do it. (Bowling is a particularly bad example. Cooper doesn't even rate it. One is left to assume that 3 lines of bowling are on a par with 4 episodes of "Laverne & Shirley".)

My own suggestion in deciding among the possibilities is to take the smorgasbord approach. Use one of the staple aerobics to build up a base of fitness, and then branch out to maintain it. The key isn't monotony, it's regularity.

13

Among the pure aerobics, those that provide the most bang for your buck, are: cycling, running, swimming and jumping rope. All four meet the basic criteria of placing a sustained moderate level stress on a number of major muscle groups while staying within the body's capacity to supply and burn oxygen (the term "aerobics" means literally "with air"). None are "sprint and stop" type activities.

If you haven't picked up a jump rope in years it may surprise you to see it included in this group. It usually takes no more than one session with a rope for this impression to wear off.

A skip rope is an exercise tool, a cheap rowing machine. With it you can elevate your pulse at a rate quick enough to warrant taking some precautions before starting on a program with it, (particularly if you're terribly out of shape, over thirty-five or have a history of heart trouble). The positive side to this is that with a jump rope, you can achieve and maintain fitness in a relatively short amount of time.

Speaking of positives, consider the following:
• Jumping rope can be done in any high ceilinged room with just a modest amount of elbow room.
• You don't have to leave the house. (Parents of small children take note).
• You've already bought all the equipment you'll ever need.
• It's totally portable (travelers take note).
• It's orthopedically easy on your feet and knees, relative to jogging.

THE LONGEST JOURNEY
STARTS WITH A SINGLE HOP

Before you jump right into your new exercise program, visions of Charles Atlas and Jane Fonda dancing in your head, I want to prepare you for the experience since you may well come away from the first session with two negative impressions.

ONE: It's exhausting.

Actually it's only surprisingly tiring, the key word being "surprisingly". Probably because of the association with playgrounds and pigtails. Think of it this way: you're not going to be jumping rope for 10 minutes, you're going to be alternately contracting and extending the two most massive muscle groups in your body while jumping up and down in coordination with with specific arm movements. It'll seem less tiring, (or at least less surprisingly so).

TWO: It's boring.

With the exception of only a couple of activities — skydiving leaps to mind — everything you're terrible at is boring. And let's face it, for a while here, you're going to be an eager, dedicated, anxious to learn, terrible rope skipper. Afterwards, once you get into the advanced steps, the boring problem will take care of itself.

How Long and How Hard

Sit down someplace and relax. Now take your pulse for 15 seconds and multiply by 4. The number you get is roughly your Resting Pulse Rate. Memorize it: it's your measure of your heart's health. (Actually, to get a more accurate figure, take your pulse first thing in the morning before breakfast, while you're still unstressed, uncaffeinated and unfed. During the day you can experience a daily range of ±15 beats per minute.)

Now imagine yourself waking up in an old rowboat drifting toward the lip of Niagara Falls. As you take up the oars you begin to experience an increase in your heart rate, probably an abrupt one. With the thunder of the falls filling your brain, you put the pedal to the cardiovascular metal, flailing away with everything you've got.

Welcome to your Maximal Heart Rate. It's a number you can approximate by subtracting your age from 210. Whatever *that* number is, multiply it by .75.

This last number is your Training Rate (±10%). It's important enough to write down in the box provided:

My Name Is _____

My Maximal Pulse Rate Is (210-my age) _____

My Training Rate Is (.75 x above) _____

My Resting Pulse Rate Is _____

My Homeroom Teacher's Name Is _____

When you're exercising near your Training Rate, you're realizing the benefits of aerobic exercise in the most

FINDING YOUR TARGET ZONE

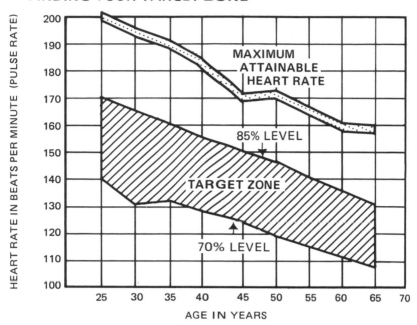

efficient manner. You *can* achieve some Training Effect at rates as low as 25% of your Maximal, but it's a far less efficient pace and one that will take a great deal more time.

On the other hand, you should *not* exercise at a rate more than 85% of your Maximal — unless you're training for the Olympics.

Note: This is not as needless a warning as it might appear. There are too many of us who can boost our pulse rate that high with an embarassingly modest amount of exertion. What it will take to get yours up to that point is something you're going to have to find out, in the following manner:

Step One: After warming up and stretching for a bit, begin skipping rope or running in place, gradually picking up the pace until you're winded enough to make conversation difficult (this may take 1 minute, it may take 5, depending). Then stop and clap your hand immediately over your heart and count for 10 seconds using a watch. You have to do this the moment you stop moving, otherwise your pulse will begin to slow down and skew your results.

Step Two: Multiply the number of beats times 6. Be as accurate as you can, if you counted 22½, include the fraction in your calculation.

If your answer is ±10% of your Training Rate figure, then you've found your exercise pace. If your result was too high or too low, try again with the appropriate adjustment in speed.

Once you've run this little experiment on yourself you can avoid the necessity of repeating it all the time by remembering the effort required. A good way to do this is to talk to yourself while you're jumping. You'll soon discover a pace at which talking is easy, one at which you'd just as soon not, and one at which you can barely think, never mind talk.

Locate your Training Rate in this spectrum, it should fall somewhere in the middle. You'll still be able to talk, but you won't be terribly chatty.

From here on in, when I'm talking about the need for 15 minutes of exercise, these are the kind of minutes I'm talking about.

Note though that you're not expected to reach and hold this pace in the program until you've had a substantial break-in period.

Your rope should come to your armpits (plus or minus a few inches) when you stand in the middle of it.

Equipment

Your Klutz Speedskip® rope is 9½ feet long, which should work fine for most people (5'5" to 6'4", more or less) but you can shorten it by pushing the knot out of one handle and re-tying it. Note though that you'll have to re-tie the knot *tightly* and clip it off *closely* so that the tail end doesn't drag in the handle and cause the rope to twist. (If you're having trouble getting the knot tight enough, step on one end and use both hands to pull).

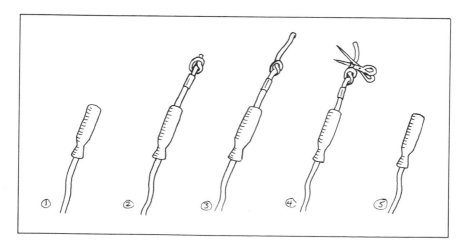

As far as jump rope attire goes, I'll leave that up to you. We're considering making available a line of designer-label Klutzwear® but as of now, it's still in the prototype stage.

I would suggest, though, that you use a pair of comfortable heel-less shoes. Running shoes are fine, but there's no use spending a pile of money on the expensive kind since you'll be buying a lot of heel padding that you won't need.

Environment

Music is the critical element, one that I can't recommend too highly (were it not for the album *Pick Hits of the 60's,* for example, you would not be reading this book). Outside of that all you'll need is a little space — mostly over your head, about 3½ feet — plus a bit of elbow room, so try to keep the crowds back.

Commitment

There are a few behavior modification tricks to help you with this (see the following section) but unfortunately there's no substitute for making The Choice.

It's a depressing fact that our health, once the exclusive responsibility of evil spirits and good kharma, has recently been dumped almost entirely into our own laps.

It used to be so much simpler. You got sick or you didn't. If you did, you went to the local healer for a cure of uncertain ingredient, never knowing from whence the

21

problem came, nor, if you were cured, where it went. But these days, particularly in the area of heart disease, our own medicine men are copping out. They're pointing fingers at us of all people, the innocent victims, and at a lifestyle that many of us have grown lovingly accustomed to. For this they make $90,000 a year?

Personally I could be very happy in a medically primitive society. I'm comfortable with the idea of scapegoats and really don't mind forces that are outside my control and understanding.

Unfortunately, neither you nor I live in such comfortingly ignorant times. We have become, perhaps unwillingly, our own physicians, and whether we self-prescribe good health care or bad is, unavoidably, our own choice.

Happy choosing.

Does The Name Pavlov Ring a Bell?

Having made your choice, a number of strategies open up for making it stick. First off, regular exercise is too important a matter to be left in the hands of your conscious brain with its handy files of excuses and plausible alibis. It's too risky. Your objective should be to sink it into the depths of your sub-conscious, down there with your instinctive reflexes.

STEP ONE: Accounting
You're going to have to keep track of your progress on paper, at least until you've gone through the 3-month program. I realize it's tedious and clinical, but if you can't show yourself how you're improving, you'll never last it out.
Keep track of the following statistics:
• Resting Pulse Rate
• Weight
• Waist
• Your biggest measurement around

A note for the weight watchers: Aerobic exercise will oftentimes tighten up your measurements without affecting your weight. It performs this little magic trick by converting fat into lean, dense muscle tissue — a very healthy turn of

events. If your scale doesn't change, but you're taking a size smaller pants, that's what's happening. See the *Jump Rope Diet* for a fuller description of this.

STEP TWO: The Rut
Create a time and place for your exercise, put it into some kind of specific place and "feel". A certain room, certain time, after something specific, before something specific . . . it doesn't matter. Just be sure to cement it into place with a lot of context.

STEP THREE: Associations
I've already mentioned music, which is a key ingredient to this.

Set aside particular clothes. On those days when your will-power is threatening to fold, you can sneak in by just "trying on" your jump rope clothes (no obligation) and then maybe "wandering" into your jump rope room, still just experimenting. And finally putting on your jump rope album.

Then let nature take its course.

You'll be amazed. It's humiliating how Pavlovian we are.

STEP FOUR: Rewards and Punishments
According to classic behavior mod theory, appropriate rewards and punishments for performance or lack thereof are critical to success. But the idea of either collecting a banana or subjecting myself to a mild electric shock every day is the place where I think I have to draw the line. People have devised less extreme stick and carrot schemes, and some have claimed great success for them. Things like dessert-witholding or no-bedtime-story-for-me-tonight.

●

But at the risk of sounding pious or self-righteous, exercise is its own reward. All the health claims aside, you'll know when your body's been warmed up and stretched out. It's a feeling of everyday celebration, the Jiminy Cricket syndrome of grinning health and groundless optimism. Once sampled, it'll have you crawling back for more.

But just in case, there's a "Do-It-Yourself/Do-It-Or-Else", self-contract in the back.

THE JUMP ROPE DIET

Owing to the dearth in recent years of published materials on the subjects of diets and dieting, I have decided to include this section in the hopes of stirring some interest in a neglected field and at the same time possibly presenting some interesting evidence on the difference between pounds actually "spent" in exercise and pounds "loaned out" on a diet.

The most popular image used when the subject of diet and exercise is brought up is the "body as bathtub" metaphor. Calories pour in by eating and out by exercise. Simple. And for the most part, quite accurate.

When the two halves of this picture are unbalanced, as they are for 50 million overweight Americans, it seems natural to attack the problem at the source, to turn down the tap.

Enter the American diet industry.

It has been, by my unofficial reckoning, more than ten years now since any women's magazine hit the stands

without a new, phenomenally successful diet within its covers. Despite their apparent fervor in trying to solve our nation's weight problem, I suspect that the real possibility of a permanently thin America would strike terror into the heart of the American publishing community.

But they need have little fear.

Last year it has been estimated that, under the guidance of some 30,000 diets, we as a nation lost some 110 million pounds — and then promptly gained them back, with a couple million in interest.

Dr. Jean Mayer of Tufts University calls it "the rhythm method of girth control", and medically speaking, it's about as reliable as its namesake.

So what's the solution?

Back to the bathtub. Time to look at the drain.

Jumping rope for 15 minutes at a Training Rate pace burns about 150 calories. Keep that up for a 3-month exercise program and you'll be out a little over 2 pounds, all of it pure fat (and that's assuming you don't change your eating habits at all).

Now I realize that 2 pounds over 3 months is chicken feed by the standards of your average wonder diet, but I submit that there is a significant difference between 2 pounds gone forever and 8 pounds out on a short-term loan.

To illustrate this point, let's assume you burn those 7000 calories jumping rope without losing a single ounce. Maybe you got a job at a doughnut shop at the same time. And then at the end of that period you quit exercising, left the doughnut shop, and went back to your old eating habits. What would happen?

You'd start losing weight.

Why? Because you replaced fat with muscle tissue, and muscle tissue burns calories — fat doesn't. Even while you're completely at rest.

After a period of inactivity, your new muscle would revert to fat and you'd be back to where you were before the whole thing started, but the lesson is this:

The 2 pounds you lost directly by exercising are just the bonus. When you replace fat with muscle, you're turning up your body's idle 24 hours a day, and you become a better calorie burning machine.

Meanwhile, a few other things are taking place. For example, you're now carrying a smaller fat load, and doing it with a couple of extra horsepower. The result? You'll start finding yourself at the tops of stairs just a little sooner, and walking down to the store suddenly won't seem quite so far. You might even drag yourself out for a game of tennis now and then.

After a while, it starts to add up. The 7000 jump rope calories become 9000 jump rope+walking+stair climbing +fooling around calories. And now you're pushing 3 pounds down, without skipping a single accustomed, incredibly caloric goodie.

Dr. Mayer, an internationally known nutritionist, puts it this way:

"Inactivity is the most important reason behind the problem of overweight in modern Western societies. The regulation of food intake was never designed for the highly mechanized, sedentary conditions of modern life. If a person is to live a sedentary life without getting fat, he will have to step up his activity level, or be hungry all his life."

None of this should be taken as an all-out defense of the standard American menu, which nearly all nutritionalists agree is both over-fatty and over-salty. Nor is it a blanket denial of the value of calorie consciousness.

A reasonable diet can serve a function — secondary to exercise, maybe — but nevertheless it can have a role in a weight-loss program.

Phenomenal claims for any wonder diet though should be given the same wide berth that phenomenal claims ought to be given most anywhere. The best-selling diets tend to emphasize speed ("Dr. Rupert Vromsky, formerly chief medical officer at Stalag 17 says, *"You'll lose 40 pounds in the first week!"*) But unless you're interested in dieting as a competitive sport, the speed factor is the least of your concerns. If it took years to put your energy in/energy out equation out of balance, it's going to take a long time to put it back in.

For the most prudent, deeply researched dietary information, you need look no further than the American Heart Association which publishes a pamphlet entitled "The Way to a Man's Heart". It may never hit the best-seller list (it's free, for one thing) but the information is solid and the focus is on the long-term, which is, after all, where you'll be spending the rest of your life.

THE FIVE BASIC STEPS

1. **Plain Old Up and Down**	3. **Rhythm Step**
2. **Skipping**	4. **Running Step**

5. Jumping Jacks

Jumping rope can be practiced on any level from the basic "rotate-jump-and-untangle" to that of a spinning dance and gymnastic routine. For the purposes of this exercise program you don't really need any but the most basic kind of steps, which I'll describe below. The advanced stuff, which can be extraordinarily challenging and fun to try, I'll describe in the appendix "Fancy Stuff". Don't hesitate to turn to it as soon as you've mastered the basics.

Plain Old Up and Down

Assuming you've gotten a proper length rope (see equipment) and are wearing comfortable heel-less shoes, try jumping over the rope with both feet at the same time, knees bent to take the shock. Use a slow motion (just enough to keep the rope fully stretched). Between each jump take a small rhythm bounce.

This is the basic "slow rope", about 60-70 turns per minute. Later on you'll use it for resting, but for now you'll need it to figure out how high you have to jump over the rope.

The answer, incidentally, is "not very far". From the beginning, unless you're deliberately trying to, you should aim to keep your jumps low. This is not a sport for kangaroos.

At the risk of being obvious, I should explain that a "fast rope" is about half again the speed of a slow rope (say about 80-90 turns per minute). You'll have no time for a rhythm bounce. Both of these tempos are usable for all the steps described.

Skipping

If you can't remember how this goes, ask the nearest 8 year old. The idea is to skip in place, jumping over the rope every time with a little one-footed hop.

Incidentally, this is a great step for moving around, running errands, changing the channel ... things like that. (The world record, for those of you interested, for travel by jump rope, is held by one Tom Morris of Australia who once covered 1,264 miles that way.)

Rhythm Step

Rocky's favorite. It won't take long doing Plain Old Up and Down or Skipping before you're ready for something a little more challenging — and this is it. You can develop this step to the point where it looks and sounds like a Fred Astaire tap dance routine.

Stand up and walk in place, on your toes, without lifting your feet more than about 6 inches off the ground.

That's the basic idea. Now all you have to do is slide your rope through it, untangling as necessary.

My guess, incidentally, is 2 weeks minimum before you can execute this very well at all, which is about the same time you should start lowering your step and moving your feet slightly forward and back for the full Muhammad Ali effect.

Running Step

A more strenuous variation of the Rhythm Step.

Jumping Jacks

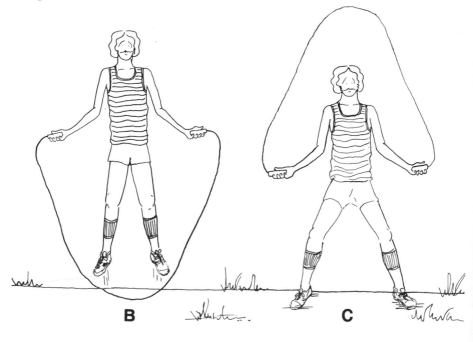

All together now . . . up . . . out . . . together again

A

B

C

34

THE PROGRAMS

The jump rope exercise programs outlined here are the heart of this book. They represent a commitment period of 12 weeks (that's 3 lunar months, one-fourth of a year, or the amount of time it would take an average snail to cover 60 miles). Out of those 12 weeks you'll be asked to commit approximately 596 minutes of it (that's about five-thousandths of 1%, 9.93 hours, or something less than about half the time you'll be spending in the bathroom).

During that period you'll lower your Resting Pulse Rate, strengthen your heart-muscle while reducing its work load, enrich your capacity to transport and burn oxygen, strengthen the two major muscle groups in your body and probably turn into a fair rope skipper. It'll be about the best 596 minutes you'll spend over the next 3 months.

The recommendations about frequency (4 times per week) and duration (15 minutes at a Training Rate pace) are made based on the American College of Sports Medicine position statement on the subject as well as studies done at the Cooper Clinic for Aerobic Research in Dallas, Texas.

A word of caution before starting in: Rope skipping is a strenuous activity quite on par with jogging or cycling. For sedentary people or those over 35, it can be highly imprudent to launch into any exercise program without a check-up. So saying I'll make the following recommendation:

If you know yourself to be badly out of shape, if you're over 35, or have any history of heart problems, get a physical. Explain that you want to start in on an exercise program and you need a green light. Ideally, go to a clinic where they can administer a stress electro-cardiogram

35

and check your heart out when it's close to its maximal rate. The information you'll get about your overall health, not only as it pertains to exercise, is something you probably owe yourself anyway.

In addition to this prime recommendation, Dr. Kenneth Cooper, director of the Aerobics Center in Dallas, Texas, issues the following recommendations and precautionary notes:

1. Proper diet, equipment and work-out conditions.
2. Adequate preliminary warm-up and stretching.
3. Correct performance objectives.
4. Adequate cool-down afterwards.
5. Frequent pulse monitorings.

And if at any time during your exercising you experience either chest pains, dizziness or nausea, you're overdoing it, a doctor's advice is indicated.

One concluding comment: Although reliable statistics are hard to come by, the number of non-cardiac patients who have suffered heart attacks while properly exercising is diminishingly small, if not nil. If you pay attention to the above advice, your chances of experiencing any cardiac ill-effects from a reasonable age-adjusted program of conditioning exercise are only slightly better than your chances of being hit by a meteorite this year.

●

RECOMMENDED PROGRAM FOR THE UNDER 30 CROWD

Note: Do not forget to warm-up and stretch for a couple of minutes before starting in every day. And at the finish, cool-down for a minute or so by walking around and shaking your arms and legs.

If you're already fairly well conditioned, you can accelerate this a bit but do so with caution. Human nature being what it is, you'll probably over-estimate your actual condition and suffer the aches and painful consequences the next morning. Start in slowly, there'll be plenty of chance to test your mettle later on.

WEEK ONE: 10 mins/day for 4 days
COMMENTS: Keep it slow. Stop whenever you need to, but keep moving around and staying warm. The time refers to combined resting and exercising. This is a break-in period. Recommended music: Guy Lombardo or Lawrence Welk.
THOUGHT FOR THE WEEK

Probably the best jump roping animal, assuming you could interest him in trying, would not be the kangaroo, who has an excellent vertical leap (40 feet plus) but is rather tall (4-5 feet), but the grasshopper who can jump approximately 15 times his own body length. Plus, he could get by with a 4" rope.

Put it all together and he ought to be able to do 30-40 turns at a hop, easy.

WEEK TWO: 10 mins/day for 4 days
COMMENTS: More or less the same pace but try to shorten or cut out the breaks. Might as well keep the same record on.
THOUGHT FOR THE WEEK

Arteriosclerosis, "hardening of the arteries", has traditionally been thought of as a disease affecting only the aged. But a study of Korean War casualties (average age 22) noted that more than 30% already showed early signs of the arteriosclerotic process.

WEEK THREE: 10 mins/day for 4 days
COMMENTS: Try to jump continuously for the full 10, using whatever pace you can hold.
THOUGHT FOR THE WEEK

Despite holding the undisputed world-record for Collective Self-Importance, human beings would be the Lichtenstein of any inter-species Olympics.

In the sprints, for example, the smart money'd be on the cheetahs. Middle distances up to 10,000 meters would probably be a good race between the antelopes and gazelles. In the pool, what with the sharks and whatnot entered, the humans would be lucky if they even finished.

Our only hope, besides basketball, would be in a new event, an *ultra* long race, 100 miles or more, where aerobic training could really pay off. Horses would be the main competition, and, based on current performance standards, they'd have to be the favorites. But not by much. The Tevis Cup, for example, is a one hundred mile horse race held annually in California. The winners usually take around 14 hours. The Western States One Hundred is a 100 mile human race also held in California annually. And the winning time there is just under 15 hours, only 9% more. (*"It's Salazar by a Nose. 'Mamma's Girl' takes the Silver."*)

38

WEEK FOUR: 13 mins/day for 4 days
COMMENTS: Same pace but it's got to be time to change
the record. Try James Taylor, Willie Nelson, or Merle
Haggard, if you can stand him.
THOUGHT FOR THE WEEK

The Average American will consume, by the age of 70,
about 55 tons of food. Partially broken down that comes to:
9 pigs, 8 cows, 15,000 eggs, 800 lbs. of fish, 6.5 tons of
bread and grain products, 2 tons of potatoes, 750 lbs. of
tomatoes, 600 lbs. of salt, 28 lbs. mustard, 700 gallons
beer, 1300 gallons soft drinks, 53 lbs. catsup, 3000 lbs.
pasta or tacos, 500 lbs. bananas and three-fourths of a ton
of candy. Yum.

WEEK FIVE: 13 mins/day for 5 days
COMMENTS: Time to establish your Training Rate. Find out what pace elevates your pulse into the 145 range (see "How Long and How Hard"). Keep as many of the 13 minutes as you can at this pace.
THOUGHT FOR THE WEEK

Unscientific study after unscientific study has shown that this period, the middle quarter, is critical in terms of final success for your whole program. The novelty has worn off, your goals have receded well over the horizon, your rate of improvement has flattened out, your friends are tired of hearing about it . . . it's a premature case of the seven-year itch.

Time to reassess your committment and review your progress.

One. Re-read the "Why Bother" section and look at Appendix C, the position statement from the American College of Sports Medicine. Reflect on the fact that coronary operations are both expensive and time consuming.

Two. Re-create your first day's workout and remember how tired it made you. Contrast it with your workout today.

Three. Buy yourself another album.

Four. Charge back in.

WEEK SIX: 13 mins/day for 5 days
COMMENTS: Same pace but you ought to be using more than just the Plain Old Up and Down. Start to work on the Rhythm Step especially.

Time for a new album. How about the early Chipmunks?
THOUGHT FOR THE WEEK

Health care in the U.S. today absorbs approximately one dollar out of every ten spent. That represents a six-fold increase over the 1965 level when Americans were, by and large, just about as healthy as they are today.

WEEKS SEVEN THROUGH ELEVEN: 15 mins/days for 5 days

COMMENTS: Welcome to your plateau week. This is the pace and duration you'll be training at for the rest of the program. It's also a good week to start getting into some of the trickier stuff, but do it on your own time. Keep the 15 to something you can do continuously.

THOUGHT FOR THE WEEKS

Launching into an exercise program frequently carries with it a certain degree of social risk. You'll often find yourself exposed to the arteriosclerotic "wit" of armchair humorists.

Actually, some of them are fairly funny, to wit:

DOONESBURY   by Garry Trudeau

MILES, LET'S TALK ABOUT THE BENEFITS OF JOG-GING NOW! THERE ARE QUITE A FEW OF THEM, AREN'T THERE? | THAT THERE ARE, MARK! I SHOULD SAY THERE ARE BENEFITS TO BEAT THE BAND! | ASIDE FROM CONDITIONING THE ALL-IMPORTANT CARDIOVASCULAR SYSTEM, JOGGING CAN IMPROVE MUSCLE TONE, CLEAR THE COM-PLEXION, AND REDUCE THE A-MOUNT OF SLEEP ONE NEEDS!

JOGGING ALSO SEEMS TO STIMU-LATE CREATIVITY. A FRIEND OF MINE WITH WRITER'S BLOCK START-ED JOGGING, AND WITHIN A MONTH HE HAD PRODUCED A PULITZER PRIZE WINNING NOVEL! | THAT'S EX-CEPTIONAL OF COURSE.. | OF COURSE. BUT MOST WRITERS DO EXPERIENCE A SHARP RISE IN TYPING SKILLS.

41

WEEK TWELVE: 15 mins/day for 5 days
COMMENTS: You've arrived at the starting line for your second program, The Big One. You can maintain this level of fitness with 4 days per week — 15 minutes per day — of Training Rate aerobic exercise for the rest of your life. You can choose from skipping rope to high speed croquet to handball to jai a'lai. I recommend a variety, depending on the season and your tastes.
THOUGHT FOR THE REST OF YOUR LIFE:

"First, be a good animal."
                    Ralph Waldo Emerson

PROGRAM FOR THE 30-39 GROUP

Note: Don't forget to warm-up and stretch for a couple of minutes before starting in every day. And at the finish, cool-down for a minute or so by walking around and shaking your arms and legs.

If you're already fairly well-conditioned, you can accelerate this a bit, but do so with caution. Human nature being what it is, you'll probably have a tendency to over-estimate and suffer the aches and painful consequences the next morning. Start in slowly, there'll be plenty of time to test your mettle later on.

WEEK ONE: 10 mins/day for 4 days
COMMENTS: Just warm-up and get used to the rope. Jump slowly (60 turns per minute), stop and rest whenever necessary, but stay loose and keep moving throughout. The time refers to your combined exercising and resting. Recommended music: The Blue Danube.
THOUGHT FOR THE WEEK

People with stubborn weight problems are understandably tempted to cite genetic or biological explanations. Will-power and a change in life-style, they reason, can't reverse what nature meant to be. Unfortunately, the facts don't bear them out.

Of the 50 million Americans who are overweight, approximately 2% owe their condition to hormonal imbalances or other organic causes.

As for genetics, the observation that overweight parents are far more likely to have overweight children than their slimmer counterparts is undeniably true, but the reasons for it are more likely found in the icebox than in the DNA.

This is a conclusion forcefully illustrated by 2 studies on the pets found in the homes of overweight owners. The researchers found that Fido was much more likely to be dragging bottom if his owners shared the same problem.

43

WEEK TWO: 10 mins/day for 4 days
COMMENTS: Still just warming up really, but try to shorten your break periods. Your basic step is the Plain Old Up and Down, but skipping and rhythm step are worth starting on.
THOUGHT FOR THE WEEK

There is very little that the U.S. Government has not taken an interest in at some time or another. I offer as conclusive evidence the Dairy Queen Cheese Dog and McDonald's Big Mac, both of which came under scrutiny by Senator George McGovern's Select Committee on Nutrition and Human Needs. The former, incidentally, contains 330 calories and 19 grams of fat, while the latter checks in with 541 calories and 31 grams of fat.

In the course of their proceedings, some of which dragged on well into the dinner hour, the committee members discovered something which came to be described as the "perfect McGovern food" since it supplies the basic nutrients in approximately the amounts recommended in the Dietary Goals. Further investigation revealed the fact that it contained a well-balanced 15 per cent protein, 27 per cent fat and 58 per cent carbohydrates. All in all, a very reasonably nutritious dish.

Thus it was that take-out pizza received the governmental stamp of approval, while the former favorite, the so-called "American hot-dog" fell onto harder times.

WEEK THREE: 12 mins/day for 4 days
COMMENTS: Try to shorten your break periods and start thinking about putting something a little more upbeat on the record player.
THOUGHT FOR THE WEEK

Although it's never been officially conferred, the title of fastest human with a jump rope might have to go to Katsuma Suzuki of Japan who once completed 51 consecutive

●

quadruple jumps (where, in a single jump, the rope passes under your feet four times). In order to execute a "quadruple", it's necessary to whip the rope around at an estimated 300 turns per minute.

The title of "Most Durable" would probably go to an American, Frank P. Oliveri, who jumped for 12 hours 8 minutes in Chicago on June 13, 1981.

WEEK FOUR: 12 mins/day for 4 days
COMMENTS: Aim for 12 non-stop minutes at your accustomed pace.
THOUGHT FOR THE WEEK

All of us know and hate individuals who can eat like horses and never gain an ounce, and others who are forced to the edge of malnutrition just to hold the line. What's surprising about these unscientific observations is that they're basically true. Study after study has shown that overweight people do not — on average — consume more calories than their slimmer counterparts.

The secret? Exercise, for the most part. Consciously taken in the form of a program, and unconsciously taken as a result of a nimbler, lighter body.

WEEK FIVE: 12 mins/day for 4 days
COMMENTS: Time to establish your Training Rate. Determine what pace will elevate your pulse into the 135 range (see "How Long and How Hard") and begin to make that pace your goal.
THOUGHT FOR THE WEEK

Unscientific study after unscientific study has shown that this period, the middle quarter, is critical in terms of final success for your whole program. The novelty has worn off, your goals have receded well over the horizon, your rate of

45

improvement has flattened out, your friends are tired of hearing about it . . . it's a premature case of the seven-year itch.

Time to reassess your committment and review your progress.

One. Re-read the "Why Bother" section and look at Appendix C, the position statement from the American College of Sports Medicine. Reflect on the fact that coronary operations are both expensive and time consuming.

Two. Re-create your first day's workout and remember how tired it made you. Contrast it with your workout today.

Three. Buy yourself another album.

Four. Charge back in.

WEEK SIX: 10 mins/day for 4 days
COMMENTS: Your goal should be 10 minutes at your Training Rate with only a few stops, (the honeymoon is over).
THOUGHT FOR THE WEEK

For years Japan has enjoyed the bottom spot among industrialized nations in terms of heart disease. While the U.S. rate is about 3 times that of Switzerland's, it is 10 times that of Japan.

However, along with blue jeans and punk, Japan has been importing some Western dietary habits. As a consequence, in 1982, Japan's incidence of heart disease jump up to 3 times what it had been 10 years ago. (On the other hand, the Japanese fondness for salt has made high blood pressure their leading cause of death and disability).

WEEK SEVEN: 12 mins/day for 4 days
COMMENTS: Same goals as last week, but a longer workout.

THOUGHT FOR THE WEEK

Although the Defense Department has looked into everything else, they seem to have ignored the possibilities of Jump Rope Warfare.

Time magazine published an intriguing article almost 20 years ago discussing the possible effects of "man-made geo-physical disturbances". The concern at the time was with the Chinese who it was thought might collectively, all 1 billion of them, climb onto little step-ladders and launch themselves off at a signal.

The resultant land mass disruption, it was thought, could have devastating effects on some of the fault systems underlying North America.

Once we'd picked ourselves up from this first strike though, the U.S. could counter-punch with a mass synchronized jump rope routine. Throw in the NATO forces and keep it going for 15 minutes or so, and it'd be a deterrent to reckon with.

WEEKS EIGHT THROUGH ELEVEN: 14 mins/day for 4 days
COMMENTS: This is the backstretch period. You ought to be getting into some of the trickier steps by now, a couple of cross-overs now and then in case someone's watching. Same pace, longer time goal.

THOUGHT FOR THE WEEK

Maximum pulse rate seems to be a relative constant among humans, reaching its highest at around 200 beats per minute in adolescents and then gradually declining with age.

Minimum pulse rate, achieved mostly by superbly conditioned athletes, is somewhere in the range of 34. A recent test among Olympic contestants found the lowest rates among the Scandianavian cross-country skiers.

Meanwhile, over in the Wild Kingdom, your average canary even when at rest, trips along at approximately 1000 beats per minute, while the sperm whale gets by on 5 or 6 per minute. Thump . . . . Thump.

WEEK TWELVE: 15 mins/day for 4 days
COMMENTS: Welcome to the starting line for your second program, The Big One. You can backslide into your former derelict ways, or you can maintain your newfound health by choosing one or another of the aerobic exercises and working out 4 days per week, 15 minutes per day at your Training Rate. For the rest of your life. Put on *Chariots of Fire.*
THOUGHT FOR THE REST OF YOUR LIFE
   "First, be a good animal."
                              Ralph Waldo Emerson

THE JUMP ROPE EXERCISE PROGRAM (40-49 years old)

Note: Don't forget to stretch and warm-up for a couple of minutes before starting in every day. And at the finish, cool-down for a bit by walking around and shaking your arms and legs.

WEEK ONE: 7 mins/day for 4 days
COMMENTS: Just warm-up and get used to the rope. Jump slowly (60 turns per minute), stop and rest as necessary, but stay loose and moving throughout. The 7 minutes refers to combined skipping and resting. Use the Plain Old Up and Down and put on a waltz.
THOUGHT FOR THE WEEK

Walter Stack is a San Francisco longshoreman who competes two or three times a year in marathons. To stay in shape, Mr. Stack routinely runs a 17 mile loop across Golden Gate Bridge every morning followed up with a half-mile swim in the Bay. It would be a remarkable routine for anyone, but it approaches the phenomenal when you consider the fact that at 75 Mr. Stack is 10 years past mandatory retirement at most corporations.

WEEK TWO: 10 mins/day for 4 days
COMMENTS: Still warming up. Try the Skip Step for some variety. Keep to your slow rope pace and rest as necessary.
THOUGHT FOR THE WEEK

In order to really find out what effect exercise has on life span, researchers would have to devise an experiment where they could isolate inactivity from the other major risk factors, i.e. high blood pressure, smoking, fatty diet and family history.

In other words, they'd need to find a population of chain smoking, overweight, hypertensive, exercise fanatics.

Needless to say, this is no easy task. The reason is that health and health awareness breeds upon itself in a "delicious cycle". Once you start exercising, you'll find yourself watching your diet and other habits automatically.

WEEK THREE: 10 mins/day for 4 days
COMMENTS: The last week of the honeymoon. Still a slow rope pace but shorten your breaks.
THOUGHT FOR THE WEEK

"By taking five simple steps, by not smoking, by using alcohol in moderation, by eating a proper diet and getting the proper amount of exercise and sleep, a 45 year old man can expect to live 10 or 11 years longer than a person who does not make these choices."
— *Richard Schweiker, formerly Secretary of Health & Human Services*

WEEK FOUR: 12 mins/day for 4 days
COMMENTS: Warm-up by trying the rhythm step but stick with your best steps for as much of the 12 minutes as possible. It must be about time to put something a little more upbeat on the record player. Benny Goodman?
THOUGHT FOR THE WEEK

Aerobic exercise, strictly administered, is frequently a staple item in rehabilitation programs for victims of stroke and heart attack. Every year the marathon circuit sees another contingent of runners who have come back from coronary recovery units.

One of the reasons for this is an effect that might be called "The Natural Coronary Bypass."

For reasons that are still the subject of research, aerobic exercise appears to foster the growth of something called "collateral vessels". In the event of a sudden blockage of arterial flow, these collaterals can "divert" enough blood around the obstruction to save your life.

WEEK FIVE: 7 mins/day for 4 days
COMMENTS: Time to figure your Training Rate. Go through the self-experiment as described in "How Long and How Hard". Once you've determined your Training Rate pace (the one that boosts your pulse into the 125 range), that becomes your pace goal. Try to keep to it for the 7 minute workout today, but take your breaks as necessary.
THOUGHT FOR THE WEEK

Unscientific study after unscientific study has shown that this period, the middle quarter, is critical in terms of final success for your whole program. The novelty has worn off, your goals have receded well over the horizon, your rate of improvement has flattened out, your friends are tired of hearing about it . . . it's a premature case of the seven-year itch.

Time to reassess your committment and review your progress.

One. Re-read the "Why Bother" section and look at Appendix C, the position statement from the American College of Sports Medicine. Reflect on the fact that coronary operations are both expensive and time consuming.

Two. Re-create your first day's workout and remember how tired it made you. Contrast it with your workout today.

Three. Buy yourself another album.

Four. Charge back in.

51

WEEK SIX: 7 mins/day for 4 days
COMMENTS: Same kind of workout as last week's.
THOUGHT FOR THE WEEK

The average American, Gallup tells us, spends 4½ hours a day watching TV — expending maybe 300 calories in the process (about equal to one Baby Ruth).

Four and a half hours is a healthy chunk of time. John McEnroe practices his tennis game less than 4½ hours a day. Barbara Streisand can make $20,000 in 4½ hours. World War III probably won't take 4½ hours.

Watching television though doesn't have to be the sedentary activity it's commonly thought as. If the average American were to push aside his easy chair and use his jump rope while putting in his 4½ hours, he'd probably develop a frightening degree of stamina while staying absolutely current with J.R. and friends.

WEEK SEVEN: 7 mins/day for 4 days
COMMENTS: Same pace and time goal as the last two weeks, but surely it must be time to change the record. *Sweet Georgia Brown?*
THOUGHT FOR THE WEEK

"Spot" reducing programs, designed to "zero-in" on thick thighs and other anatomical excesses are hardly better than exercise quackery. Unfortunately you can't isolate and draw down a fat reserve with that kind of precision.

This is not to say that aerobic exercise will not tighten up your measurements. It most certainly will. It's just that the effects will be a bit more general. All your measurements will shrink — some more than others perhaps — but your body has a percentage of fat that exercise draws upon more or less uniformly.

52

WEEK EIGHT: 10 mins/day for 4 days
COMMENTS: Same pace, but a longer day. By this time you ought to be reasonably adept at the 5 basic steps and thinking about working on some of the trickier stuff for a long term challenge (but do it on your own time). Save the workout for as continuous a run as you can do.
THOUGHT FOR THE WEEK

Exercise longer rather than harder if your goal is to really improve your fitness level. Once you're into your Training Range, your rate of return sharply diminishes as you force your pulse rate up.

For the best results, just lengthen your sessions while keeping your pulse near your Training Rate.

WEEK NINE: 10 mins/day for 4 days
COMMENTS: Same kind of workout as last week's, but you might start throwing a few moves into your act. Maybe a crossover or two if someone's watching?
THOUGHT FOR THE WEEK

Modern homemakers, according to a 1974 study, put in about 56 hours a week in house-related work, covering approximately 50 miles in the process and burning something like 12,000 calories. They are understandably indignant whenever the words "inactive" or "sedentary" are used to describe their lifestyle. (An interesting aside: A similar study done in 1924 concluded that homemakers 50 years ago spent slightly less time on house-related work than they do now. A breakdown of both studies further revealed that the modern homemaker spends more time on laundry than did her cold water and washtub equipped grandmother.)

Unfortunately housework shares the same defect that most manual labor does in term of cardiovascular benefits: it is neither strenuous nor continuous enough to elevate the pulse rate adequately.

53

Moving bags of groceries, baskets of laundry, and station wagonfuls of families around might be exhausting, frustrating, irritating and wretchedly underpaid — but it is not an aerobic exercise.

WEEK TEN: 12 mins/day for 4 days
COMMENTS: Same pace but slightly longer.
THOUGHT FOR THE WEEK

At least 17 studies have been done and published in the academic literature focused specifically on the jump rope. They include:

• A 1940 study done in Kansas City in which it was indicated that rope skipping "promoted rhythm and had masculine appeal."

• A 1969 study on high school boys showed a "marked improvement in cardiovascular efficiency", as did a 1962 study on older women.

Taken as a whole, the research serves to confirm the fact that rope skipping is an extraordinarily efficient heart conditioner (although one study did note that it seems to have a negligible effect on badminton skills).

WEEK ELEVEN: 13 mins/day for 4 days
COMMENTS: A little longer still.
THOUGHT FOR THE WEEK

If you could lower your Resting Pulse Rate by 10 beats per minute, over the course of a year, your heart will beat some 5.2 million fewer times.

Owing to the difficulties of devising large enough controlled experiments, medical science can't ultimately prove that this will lengthen your heart's life, but if you were in the market for a transplant, which one would you choose?

WEEK TWELVE: 15 minutes/day for 4 days
COMMENTS: Welcome to the start of your second program, The Big One. If you can skip rope almost continuously for 15 minutes at your training rate you are in good shape by anybody's definition. You can maintain it for the rest of your life by keeping to a 4 per week schedule, 15 minutes per workout with any aerobic activity of your choosing. Just make sure your pulse rate stays elevated and near your Training Rate for the duration of the workout.

   Congratulations. Put on *Chariots of Fire.*
THOUGHT FOR THE REST OF YOUR LIFE
"First, be a good animal."
                    Ralph Waldo Emerson

THE JUMP ROPE EXERCISE PROGRAM (50-59 years old)

Note: Don't forget to stretch and warm-up for a couple of minutes before starting in every day. And at the finish, cool-down for a bit by walking around and shaking your arms and legs.

WEEK ONE: 5 mins/day for 3 days
COMMENTS: Just warm-up and get used to the rope. Use a slow pace, 60 turns per minute, and stop as often as necessary, but stay loose and moving throughout. The 7 minutes refers to combined skipping and resting. Use the Plain Old Up and Down and put on a waltz. Don't worry if you end up skipping one minute and walking around six, you've got to start somewhere.
THOUGHT FOR THE WEEK

Aerobic exercise, strictly administered, is frequently a staple item in rehabilitation programs for victims of stroke and heart attack. Every year the marathon circuit sees another contingent of runners who have come back from coronary recovery units.

One of the reasons for this is an effect that might be called "The Natural Coronary Bypass."

For reasons that are still the subject of research, aerobic exercise appears to foster the growth of something called "collateral vessels". In the event of a sudden blockage of arterial flow, these collaterals can "divert" enough blood around the obstruction to save your life.

WEEK TWO: 5 mins/day for 3 days
COMMENTS: Still just warming up. Try the Skip Step for variety. Keep to your slow rope pace and rest as necessary.

THOUGHT FOR THE WEEK

"Stretching," according to Bob Anderson, author of a book on the subject, "is the important link between the sedentary life and the active life. It keeps the muscles supple, prepares you for movement, and helps you make the daily transition from inactivity to vigorous activity without undue strain."

There is one over-riding rule regarding a preliminary stretching — take it slow. If you're doing it correctly, it shouldn't hurt.

WEEK THREE: 7 mins/day for 3 days
COMMENTS: Same pace but a slightly longer day.
THOUGHT FOR THE WEEK

The coronary bypass operation is the surgical response to the problems of diet and exercise discussed in much of this book. It is a procedure whereby an obstructed coronary artery is bypassed with a section of new vessel, usually taken from the leg.

In 1980 more than 10,000 of these operations were performed, with a collective price tag of over $2 billion. Taking a purely commercial point of view, this is an enviable growth rate, given the fact that 20 years ago it was strictly an experimental procedure with negligible revenues.

The business analogy is not entirely out of line either, since many bypass operations are elective surgery, there's an element of marketing involved. For 10-15% of the candidates, with specific forms of obstruction, nearly everyone agrees the operation has "survival value" (it can extend your life). For another percentage, suffering from disabling chest pains, surgery may offer the only avenue of escape. But for a significant percentage of candidates, the entire procedure may be an expensive, life-threatening, internal, nose-job.

57

To quote from Dr. Robert Frye, of the Mayo Clinic and chairman of the committee organized by the National Institute of Health to study bypass operations: "There is no evidence of improved survival after surgery in patients with single vessel disease . . ."

WEEKS FOUR THROUGH EIGHT: 10 mins/day for 4 days
COMMENTS: This is a plateau period. Time to consolidate your gains and improve your skipping. By the end of it you should be jumping for at least half of the ten minutes, but bring yourself along slowly.

THOUGHT FOR THE WEEK

Unscientific study after unscientific study has shown that this period, the middle quarter, is critical in terms of final success for your whole program. The novelty has worn off, your goals have receded well over the horizon, your rate of improvement has flattened out, your friends are tired of hearing about it . . . it's a premature case of the seven-year itch.

Time to reassess your committment and review your progress.

One. Re-read the "Why Bother" section and look at Appendix C, the position statement from the American College of Sports Medicine. Reflect on the fact that coronary operations are both expensive and time consuming.

Two. Re-create your first day's workout and remember how tired it made you. Contrast it with your workout today.

Three. Buy yourself another album.

Four. Charge back in.

WEEK NINE: 12 mins/day for 4 days
COMMENTS: Still just building up.

THOUGHT FOR THE WEEK

Calisthenics can strengthen muscles, improve flexibility and burn calories, but unless they're continuous and of sufficient duration, they do not have beneficial effects on cardiovascular fitness. This is not to say that they're unneeded, just that calisthenics and aerobics do different things for your body and you should mix them into your routine according to your goals.

WEEK TEN: 12 mins/day for 4 days
COMMENTS: Last week at the slow rope pace. Savor it.
THOUGHT FOR THE WEEK

Osteoporosis is the medical term for a condition of weakened bones leading to "Dowager's hump", hip fractures and shortened stature — hallmarks of late to middle age that were previously thought unavoidable. There exists today however a significant body of research to suggest that, while it seems to be resistant to cure, osteoporosis may be preventable with healthly long-term doses of exercise and proper diet, including adequate amounts of calcium.

One study indicated that a daily hour-long walk was an effective preventative, while another demonstrated that an athlete's bones are significantly denser than those of his more sedentary counterpart.

WEEK ELEVEN: 5 mins/day for 3 days
COMMENTS: End of the honeymoon. Time to determine your Training Rate. Follow the steps in the little self-experiment described in "How Long and How Hard". Establish the pace you need to elevate your pulse rate into the 110 range. This becomes your pace goal, it'll probably be in the 80 turns per minute. Hold to it for today's shortened workout as much as you can.

59

THOUGHT FOR THE WEEK

Are you ever too old to exercise?

With rare exceptions, and subject to medical supervision, the answer is no. At the Andrus Gerontology Center of the University of Southern California, a group of retired men and women ranging in age from 52 to 88 were recruited for a study of the effects of vigorous exercise. After thorough physicals, they all began a 3 hour per week exercise program. Six weeks later, in a subjective evaluation, the majority of the group said they felt "ten to twenty years younger."

WEEK TWELVE: 5 mins/day for 4 days
COMMENTS: Same kind of workout as last week's.
THOUGHT FOR THE WEEK

Although it's never been officially conferred, the title of fastest human with a jump rope might have to go to Katsuma Suzuki of Japan who once completed 51 consecutive quadruple jumps (where, in a single jump, the rope passes under your feet four times). In order to execute a "quadruple", it's necessary to whip the rope around at an estimated 300 turns per minute.

The title of "Most Durable" would probably go to an American, Frank P. Oliveri, who jumped for 12 hours 8 minutes in Chicago on June 13, 1981.

WEEK THIRTEEN: 7 mins/day for 4 days
COMMENTS: Same pace, but a longer day. By this time you ought to have branched out and tried all five of the basic steps. Plain Old Up and Down can get pretty old all by itself.

THOUGHT FOR THE WEEK

Some international health statistics:
• Life Expectancy. Sweden is number one with 72.07 years, while the U.S. is fifteenth at 68.70.
• Physicians per capita. Albania is winner here, although there might be some question as to what constitutes an Albanian doctor. Whatever it is, they have 1 for every 159 inhabitants.
• Sweden spends $582 a year on each of its citizens for health care, the most of any country. The U.S. spends $218.
• The U.S. has 338 heart disease deaths per 100,000 inhabitants. Mozambique, on the other hand, has 3.
• Here in the U.S. we eat (on average) 3,300 calories per day. In Haiti, the figure is 1,730.

WEEK FOURTEEN: 7 mins/day for 4 days
COMMENTS: Same kind of workout as last week.
THOUGHT FOR THE WEEK

According to the American Heart Association, there is no such thing as a "sudden heart attack". A "myocardial infarction" (as they say in the biz) is the endpoint of a long term series of abuses and is frequently preceded by a number of unheeded symptoms, e.g. pain, either centered over the chest or radiating outwards; uncomfortable pressure located in the chest; dizziness; shortness of breath; palpitations; cold sweat or unexplained paleness or nausea.

WEEK FIFTEEN: 10 mins/day for 4 days
COMMENTS: Same kind of workout pace, but for an extra three minutes. Use your warmup time as an opportunity to work on some of the fancier stuff. A couple of crossovers now and then can do a lot to upgrade an act.

THOUGHT FOR THE WEEK

It's been estimated that over the course of a lifetime, your heart will pump enough blood to fill 13 supertankers. That amounts to an energy expenditure of 26,280 BTU's.

Think of it this way: If our hearts ran on gasoline rather than tuna salad sandwiches, the U.S. would need to import an extra 660 million barrels of oil every year.

WEEK SIXTEEN: 12 mins/day for 4 days
COMMENTS: Welcome to the starting gate for your next program, The Big One. Being able to jump rope fairly continuously for 12 minutes at your training pace is both your graduation ceremony and your Commencement. You can maintain this level of fitness by working out at your Training Rate, in any aerobic of your choosing or any variety, at the pace of 4 days per week, 12 minutes per day. You can do this for the rest of your life, although once past the age of 60, a doctor's specific ok is mandatory for any activity as strenuous as jogging, swimming, or jumping rope.
THOUGHT FOR THE REST OF YOUR LIFE
"First, be a good animal."
— *Ralph Waldo Emerson*

APPENDIX A: Fancy Stuff

1. The Cross-Over
2. The Cross-Step
3. The Double Jump
4. The Matador Cross
5. Side-Tapping
6. 180° Turn
7. Two-on-a-Rope
8. Can-Can
9. The Mega-Tangle

A   B   C

The Crossover

Probably the best-known little bit of razzle-dazzle you can throw into your act. The secret is to get your hands up by your armpits, as per the illustration.

When you first try this you probably won't open the rope wide enough and you'll end up lashing your ankles together. Relax and concentrate on getting your hands up rather than whipping the rope. (Incidental note: Because of the way your arms are attached, this trick is actually quite a bit easier backwards. See #6, the 180° turn.)

With patience you'll eventually get this one. And when you do, try doing multiples of it in a row.

The Cross-Step

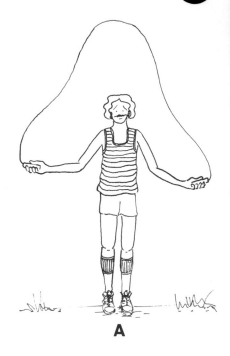

A

B

C

64

The Double-Jump

This trick takes some real speed. You'll have to get the rope up to about 150 rpm and then get extra high off the ground while you pass the rope under your feet twice before you hit the ground. Note though that you only have to pass the rope around your body a mere 1½ times (you may have to think about that one for a minute).

After you can do one, there's no *theoretical* reason why you can't do multiples in a row.

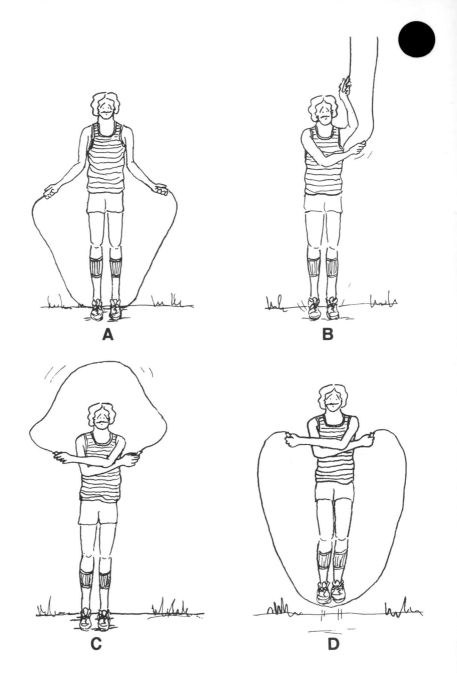

A   B

C   D

The Matador Cross

Anything I could say about this would only confuse you more, so just look at the illustrations and pray. (Note that

E

F

G

H

you only have to jump once for every three rope turns. Easy on the feet.)

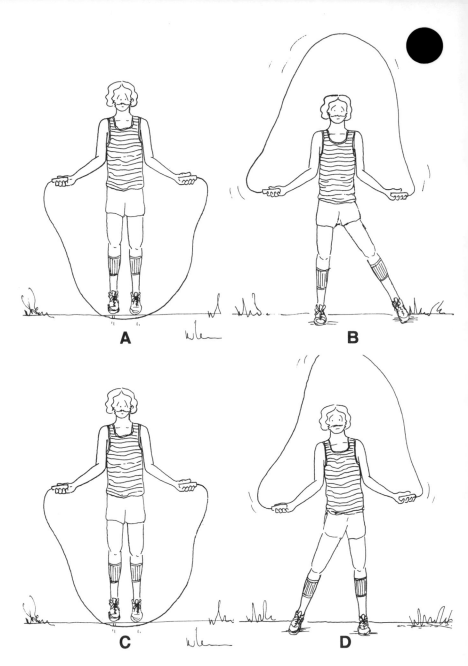

A

B

C

D

Side Tapping

This is really just a variation of the rhythm step, except that it requires a slightly higher degree of your "rubbing-tummy-while-patting-head" abilities.

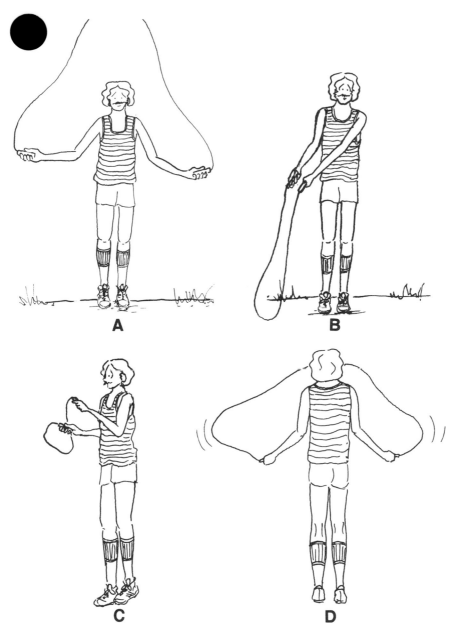

A

B

C

D

180° Turn

By itself, this is the simplest trick, but the idea is to use it in coordination with everything else. So you have Backwards Crossovers, Backwards Cross-Steps, Backwards Matador Crosses, etc.

Two-On-A-Rope

All you need is the right kind of partner and a little bit of rhythm.

A

B

C

Can-Can

Another head-patting tummy-rubber. While you're jumping on one leg, the other is doing the Rockettes thing. And then switch. Not easy.

APPENDIX B: The Do-It-Yourself/Do-It-Or-Else Exercise Contract

Whereas, the party of the first part, hereafter referred to as "the Jumper", recognizing a near-total lack of self-discipline, does hereby convey and confer certain unspecified "rights of authority" to a second party, hereafter referred to as "the Enforcer".

And, whereas the Jumper, further recognizing a criminal need for physical conditioning, does hereby agree to the following contractual conditions:

1. The Jumper will follow through on his/her prescribed jump rope exercise program for the required three (3) month period.

2. The Jumper will log his/her pulse rate, weight and measurements weekly.

3. The Jumper will eat 3 sensible meals a day, none of which may contain any ingredient incorporating the words "lip-smacking", "crunchy" or "family-pleasin' ".

The Jumper further agrees to sign and present this document to the Enforcer who may then proceed to exercise his Rights of Authority in whatever manner he may deem humane, or failing that, appropriate.

_____

First Party

_____

Second Party

APPENDIX C: Position Statement of the American College of Sports Medicine

Increasing numbers of persons are becoming involved in endurance training activities and thus, the need for guidelines for exercise prescription is apparent.

Based on the existing evidence concerning exercise prescription for healthy adults and the need for guidelines, the American College of Sports Medicine makes the following recommendations for the quantity and quality of training for developing and maintaining cardio-vasculatory fitness and body composition in the healthy adult:

1. **Frequency of training:** 3 to 5 days per week.

2. **Intensity of training:** 60% to 90% of maximum heart rate reserve or, 50% to 85% of maximum oxygen uptake.

3. **Duration of training:** 15 to 60 minutes of continuous aerobic activity. Duration is dependent on the intensity of the activity: thus lower intensity activity should be conducted over a longer period of time. Because of the total fitness effect and the fact that it is more readily attained in longer duration programs, and because of the potential hazards and compliance problems associated with high intensity activity, lower to moderate intensity activity of longer duration is recommended for the non-athletic adult.

4. **Mode of activity:** Any activity that uses large muscle groups, that can be maintained continuously, and is rhythmical and aerobic in nature, e.g. running-jogging, walking-hiking, swimming, rope-skipping, bicycling, rowing, skating, cross-country skiing and various endurance game activities.

THE KLUTZ PRESS **FLYING APPARATUS CATALOG**

Klutz Press is a specialist in the field of gravity defiance systems, and *Pumping Plastic* is actually our third venture into it. In 1977 we published *Juggling for the Complete Klutz*, and its subsequent success has enabled a nation of klutzes to finally learn the meaning of pride.

In 1982 we published *The Hacky Sack Book* describing a game that combines soccer and juggling.

Both books share a unique feature: they're packaged with the tools of their respective trades. In the case of *Juggling for the Complete Klutz,* three calico/denim bean bags are put together with the book. They're hand-sized, practically indestructible, and they won't roll away when you drop them.

As for *The Hacky Sack Book,* it comes with an official Hacky Sack footbag, a small, leather bean bag that's designed for a lifetime of foot-propelled flying.

Both of these books, as well as additional copies of *Pumping Plastic,* are available through the mail (or you can find them at your local bookstore). We also make available Hacky Sack footbags, as well as a whole raft of assorted juggling appliances (and most of these you *can't* find at your local store).

Use the blanks opposite to order.

1. **PUMPING PLASTIC: The Jump Rope**   **$9.50**
   Fitness Plan

   The subjects of health, diet, jumping rope, human anatomy and medical science will never be the same. John Cassidy and Diane Waller, with their characteristic disregard for normal standards of English communication, have written and illustrated yet another book. This one following close on the heels of the best-selling *Hacky Sack Book* and *Juggling for the Complete Klutz.* Comes complete with one vinyl, ball-bearing equipped Klutz Speedskip® rope.

2. **Klutz Speedskip® Jump Rope**   **$7.50**

   The only easily adjustable ball bearing jump rope available. Made of high-impact plastic handles steel ball-bearings, and a vinyl ¼" rope. Comes 10½ feet long.

3. **Juggling for the Complete Klutz**   **$9.50**

   The most popular book on juggling ever published. A 65 page volume, written for the mashed-finger and dented-shin crowd. By John Cassidy & B.C. Rimbeaux. Illustrated by Diane Waller. Comes with three denim and calico juggling bags.

4. **Juggling Bags**   **$1.75 ea. (set of 3/$5.00)**

   Colorful, hand-sewn bean bags of calico and denim . . . ideal size and weight for juggling. They don't bounce around, they won't roll away, and they won't make a mess on the floor. No klutz is complete without them.

5. **Juggling Pins**   **$21.50**

    Three white, injection molded polyethylene jug-
    gling pins. Basically the same shape as bowling
    pins except they're balanced and designed for
    juggling. Totally indestructible.

6. **Juggling Balls**   **$8.50**

    Three lacrosse-style, hard rubber balls with a
    ribbed, easy-to-grip surface. Each set contains
    one red, one blue and one yellow ball.

7. **Professional Style Pins**   **$47.50**

    For the semi-serious juggler. Polyethylene con-
    struction, with a padded knob, bottom, extra length
    cushioned handle and a two-toned gold and white
    finish. Barnum and Bailey material.

8. **Ultimate Juggling Bags**   **$7.00 per set of three**

    Sewn with crushed red velour (instead of calico
    and denim). Appropriate for most formal occasions

9. **Juggling Rings**   **$22.50**

    Three colorful ABS plastic juggling rings (outside
    diameter 13", inside diameter 11½", ½" thick).
    Sergei Ignatov, the Reggie Jackson of juggling,
    always uses rings when keeping more than 11
    objects going at once. Each set contains one red,
    one blue and one yellow ring.

10. **The Hacky Sack Book**   **$9.00**

A 72 page how-to book on the fine art of Hacky Sack footbag games. Written by the same crew as produced the best-selling *Juggling for the Complete Klutz.* Packaged with one Hacky Sack footbag.

11. **Hacky Sack Footbags**   **$7.00**

Thirty-two gram, hand-stitched, all leather, fully-patented, human-powered, anti-gravity devices. Used in the New American Footbag Games. Designed for a lifetime of foot-propelled flying.

12. **The Juggling Book by Carlo**   **$7.00**

The definitive work. In-depth descriptions of advanced tricks and passing patterns written by a professional juggler. For the serious (or aspiring to be serious) juggler this 102 page manual leaves no stone unturned.

MAIL ORDER BLANK

Quantity	Description	Price (includes tax, postage & handling)
Total Enclosed (check or money order)		

Name _____

Street _____

Address _____

_____

Klutz Enterprises/Box 2992/Stanford, CA 94305

Please include check or money order and mail to:
Klutz Enterprises/Box 2992/Stanford, CA 94305

MAIL ORDER BLANK

Quantity	Description	Price (includes tax, postage & handling)
	Total Enclosed (check or money order)	

Name _____

Street _____

Address _____

_____

Klutz Enterprises/Box 2992/Stanford, CA 94305

Please include check or money order and mail to:
Klutz Enterprises/Box 2992/Stanford, CA 94305